Table of Contents

Introduction

I want to thank you and congratulate you for downloading this book *"Stocks: How to Invest for Success to Make Money"*.

This book contains proven steps and strategies on how to profit from day trading.

A form of speculation, day trading is transacting financial instruments in one trading day. This means that every trading position which had been opened at the beginning of the trading day will be closed by the day trader before the financial market closes for the day. Anyone who does this with the primary purpose of generating profit is also known as a speculator. Financial instruments commonly traded in day trading include commodity futures, equity index futures, interest rate futures, stocks, currencies, and options.

Today, even the common homemaker can dabble in day trading due to the emergence of margin trading and electronic trading. Previously, only large banks and investment firms could practice day trading. Although most financial planners advise their clients that the latter would ensure that their wealth will grow over time and that it is risky to try get-rich-quick schemes, day trading can still be profitable if and when traders find the time to study the trade before trying it.

Day trading can be a crazy endeavor. A lot of day traders have to stare at their computer screens to monitor the price movements of their chosen financial asset. They have to decide quickly because they make more money when they take advantage of a lot of trades with small profits. They face limited risks because they need to close all open positions at the end of the trading session. They don't have to worry about things that may happen while they sleep that affect their current profits. However, they also have limited profits because they have to dispose their inventory daily.

I encourage you to share this book with your friends and family, and please take the time to write a short review on Amazon to share your thoughts.

Chapter 1: Terms Commonly Used In Day Trading

Broker - a person or a firm that acts as a facilitator between stakeholders.

Closing Out - the act of completing every trading transaction before the trading day ends. In most cases, day traders close all open positions in order to lessen the risk brought about by keeping the positions open overnight.

Derivative - a type of security which is dependent on the price of an underlying asset. Example: futures contracts.

Index - an imaginary collection of securities which represents a particular financial market. Example: Standard & Poor's 500.

Initial Public Offering - the initial sale of a firm's share of stock.

Leverage - the use of money borrowed from a broker for the purpose of generating more profits.

Liquidity - the ability to transact an asset in a way that doesn't affect its price.

Penny - the smallest price movement of a stock trade which serves as profit measurement.

Pip - the smallest price movement of a foreign currency pair and is often equal to 1/100 of a cent.

Point - a percentage of price movement. A point is equal to 1 penny. A point is also equal to 1% change in the price of bonds. A basis point, on the other hand, is 0.0001 or .01%.

Securities - assets that have value and can be traded in a financial market. Examples: bonds and shares of stock.

Stock - a kind of security that offers the holder the right to own a corporation.

Stockholder - a person or firm which owns shares of stock of a corporation.

Teeny - equal to 1/16 of a dollar. This is primarily the increment used in trading derivatives and bonds.

Tick - a trading increment used in futures trading. However, the measurement varies depending on the product. 1 tick is $12.50 in an E-mini Standard & Poor's 500 contract at the Chicago Mercantile Exchange. It is equal to $1.25 in an E-mini soybean contract at the Chicago Board of Trade. The tick size is often stated on the websites of those offering the exchange.

Trade - to transact a financial asset in its market through buying or selling.

Trader - a person who transacts financial assets. He is a person who holds the assets for a shorter period than an investor.

Volatility - the variance in the price of security over time.

Chapter 2: The Basics of Day Trading

Day trading isn't investing. A trader doesn't buy a financial asset with the purpose of keeping it for a long period of time to build profits. Although long-term can be subjective, an investor usually holds an asset for years. Also, the investor makes an effort to study the assets he invests in. He searches for businesses that have the capability to make a solid performance each year. On the other hand, a day trader completes the transaction in one trading day. Most of the time, he uses borrowed money to trade highly liquid indexes or stocks in order to take advantage of small movements in the price of the asset. A day trader and an investor follow the same principle. They buy assets at a low price and sell them at a high price.

Chapter 3: How Day Trading Came About

Day trading only became popular in recent years. However, there were events in the past that paved the way for its evolution.

In 1867, the development of the ticker tape made it easier for brokers to communicate transaction information on the trading floor. Traders have to go through brokers to place orders. In 1971, the NASDAQ was formed as an electronic communication network, which acts as facilitator of financial trades outside of the different stock exchanges. By 1975, fixed commissions were abolished by the Securities and Exchange Commission (SEC) to pave the way for discounted commission rates.

The SEC established the Small Order Entry System to prioritize orders less than 1,000 shares in 1987. This was SEC's answer to the problem brought about by firms that shut out small traders during the stock market crash. With the popularity of the dot-com bubble in 1997, some companies launched online trading. Small traders were able to directly access trading activities and price quotes. In 1999, then-SEC Chairman Arthur Levitt testified before Congress about day trading. This single act made day trading popular. However, the negative effects of day trading were also magnified.

In 2000, changes were made on the Small Order Entry System so that day traders no longer enjoyed some advantages. With the collapse of the stock market, a lot of day traders became bankrupt and sought other careers. In 2008, a new breed of professional day traders came to trade. These traders pursued day trading with great care and diligence.

Chapter 4: What Is Arbitrage?

A day trader usually makes small profits in a trading day. If he wants to earn more money, he can take advantage of arbitrage, a strategy that generates profits from the price discrepancies of a financial asset. Of French origin, the word arbitrage means judgment and an arbitrageur is a person who engages in arbitrage.

The basic assumption in a financial market is that the current market price is the correct price. Only long-term investors see the differences between the investment's true worth and its market price. For all other individuals, it's the market price that matters. According to the one price law, the value of the financial asset is constant everywhere. This means that the differences in price of a particular asset are only short-lived because traders will immediately cause a change by buying low and selling high.

If there is a discrepancy in the value of the financial asset among the different financial markets worldwide, the strategy is to sell the financial asset in the high-priced financial market and immediately buy the financial asset in the low-priced financial market. Theoretically, there is no risk in arbitrage because a financial asset will usually have a single price across different financial markets. Anyone who uses the arbitrage strategy doesn't risk his investments at all. However, a lot of traders and investors are seeking the same opportunity, therefore there aren't a lot of good opportunities anymore.

Chapter 5: Who is a Day Trader?

A day trader can't be a good one without the necessary personality traits and access to resources. He must understand the financial market he's dealing with. A good day trader spends a great deal of time doing research. He makes use of his broker's services, as well as other resources to know the sentiments of the market. It takes years of experience and market knowledge to be a successful day trader.

A day trader doesn't really need a lot of capital because he can borrow money from his broker. Leveraging is risky yet it has become a necessity for a day trader to increase his potential profits. A day trader also needs to craft a solid business plan because day trading is actually a business in itself. He must be able to have short and long term trading goals. He must also consider metrics, reporting, taxation, capital reinvestment, setup needs, trading time, and target markets.

A day trader is also disciplined. He must make it a point not to act on impulse. He must be able to keep his emotions in check whenever he's trading. A day trader is someone with the discipline to close all his open transactions at the end of the trading day. He is knowledgeable about limit and stop orders, as well as risk capital. A day trader is also adept with technology because trading often occurs in electronic communication networks that must be accessed through a computer with a robust Internet connection. He is also a person who makes use of different applications to gather information, as well as to execute trades.

A person who wants to be successful in day trading must be sure to have the needed resources and personality traits. He must also be willing to go through a difficult learning curve. Experienced day traders often trade professionally. It is a full-time work although it is also possible to dabble into day trading part time.

Chapter 6: On Becoming A Pattern Day Trader

A lot of day traders don't profit from their trading activities. In most cases, their losses are magnified due to leveraging. If there are more day traders who can't pay their loans to their broker, then it will greatly affect the industry. The Financial Industry Regulatory Authority (FINRA) sets rules for its members to follow in order to keep the industry afloat. Its NASD Rule 2520 pertains to day traders by setting minimum size and margin requirements for the trading account. Actually, the rules are stricter for day trading because it has greater risks.

A pattern day trader has been defined by FINRA as someone who trades at least 4 times in 5 trading days. However, if the trader's day trading transactions only constitute less than 6% of his total trades, he isn't considered a pattern day trader. On the other hand, the National Futures Association doesn't have any special definition because futures trading is basically short-term in nature.

A pattern day trader can have 25% margin account. This means that he can borrow at most 75% of the price of the financial asset he intends to trade, although some traders are only allowed 50% of the total cost of the asset. A pattern day trader must close his open positions by the end of the trading day. This will bring about less risk to the broker. A pattern day trader must sign a contract stating that he understands the risks of leveraging and that his broker can sell his financial assets in case he can't pay his loans.

NASD Rule 2520 further states that the pattern day trader must invest at least $25,000 to his trading account. If he suffers losses and wipes out his investments, then he must be sure to deposit more money so that he can continue with his day trading activities. If there is no deposit made, he can no longer borrow money and has to use cash in his trades.

FINRA has set minimum requirements; therefore, it is up to the broker to set other requirements to manage risks on his part.

Chapter 7: Important Day Trading Markets

A day trader must choose his financial market well. He must be able to concentrate in at most two markets to be successful. By specializing in a few markets, he will be able to learn the ins and outs of those financial markets, thereby allowing him to make better trading decisions. Popular financial markets include futures, forex, and stocks.

A futures agreement is basically a contract between two parties to execute a particular trade at a particular price and date in the future. Often, commodities like steer hides, rubber, precious metals, metals, textiles, fibers, oils, fats, and foods are the objects in a futures contract in order to mitigate risk and uncertainty. Financial futures, on the other hand, involve market indexes like the Dow Jones Industrial Average or the Standard & Poor's 500. In essence, a day trader dealing with financial futures bets that an index will reach a specific level at a specific future date.

The foreign exchange market is also of interest to a day trader because it is a market full of opportunities because of its wide reach and scope. The forex market trades for 24 hours, 6 times a week. A day trader can profit from the small variances in exchange rates. In order to make a lot of profit, he makes use of leveraging offered by his broker.

Another popular choice among day traders is the stock market. A day trader usually sets his sights on NASDAQ stocks because the stock exchange has more publicly listed companies. He finds a lot of trading opportunities at NASDAQ because it is also very volatile.

There are two factors that day traders consider in deciding which financial market to trade in: volatility and liquidity. Volatility is the measure of price variance of a particular asset over time. A highly volatile financial asset will have a price which fluctuates a lot. It is a primary consideration for day trading because the intra-day movements can be profitable to a day trader.

Liquidity, on the other hand, is the ability to transact the financial asset without affecting its price. It means that the financial asset can be easily traded many times in a single trading day.

Chapter 8: Techniques Used In Day Trading

Leverage

A day trader must use strategy if he wants to increase his potential earnings. Through the use of leverage, it is possible to earn more money from day trading. Leverage only increases the profits, but not the trade's performance. A day trader takes advantage of a margin account being offered by his broker if he wants to use leveraging in his trades. In most cases, this kind of account requires an initial deposit of a minimum of $2,000 USD. If the day trader opens a margin account, then his broker can lend him a maximum of 50% of his stock purchase price.

Short Selling

A day trader can also short sell. This strategy involves the day trader borrowing a financial asset from his broker and selling it. He will then buy it before the trading session ends when the price of the financial asset is cheaper. Before short selling, he must first investigate the financial market and search for an asset that has a price which is continuously going down. He then places a sell order, and borrows from his broker. Once the asset is loaned to the day trader, the sell order is executed. When the price of the asset goes down further, the day trader buys the asset and returns it to the broker. The price difference is retained by the trader as profit.

Margin Call

It is possible for the day trader to lose his money through leveraging and short selling. A margin call poses a big problem to a day trader. It is made when the margin account reaches the preset limit. If it is issued, then the day trader must add more money to his trading account. The broker has the right to sell his financial assets in order for him to stay above the limit.

Stop-Loss

To minimize the risks, he must use a stop-loss, which is an order to sell the financial asset when its price has reached the preset limit. This means that the trader need not monitor his asset's performance because he is assured that the system will sell it as soon as the preset limit has been reached. The problem with this strategy is that it will be triggered even if it's just a short-term price fluctuation.

Chapter 9: The Risks and Rewards of Day Trading

The collapse of the stock market in 2000 didn't end the trading careers of day traders. In the US Occupational Outlook Handbook in 2006, the Department of Labor estimated that there are about 320,000 financial services, commodities, and securities agents. This number includes financial service advisors, investment bankers, floor brokers, stock brokers, and day traders. However, it is difficult to ascertain the actual number of day traders.

A day trader can earn a lot of money. However, he must also be ready to suffer huge financial losses at the start of his trading career. Day trading is both expensive and extremely stressful. Also, for a trader to succeed, he must be able to screen information he can use in his day trading activities. A person who easily gets intimidated may not find satisfaction in day trading. He may, however, find success in other traditional investments.

Chapter 10: When to Consider Day Trading as a Career

A lot of day traders are also into long-term investments because most of their profits are placed into them for safety. It's actually a smart risk management strategy for a business as risky as day trading. If a short-term trader can invest in long-term goals, then a long-term investor can also trade on a short-term basis. This is possible because of three reasons:

The Investment Has a Short Life

In most cases, a long-term investor buys an investment with the intention of keeping it for a longer period. However, he may be forced to sell after a few days or weeks if his investment makes a turnaround. It can happen that the firm in which he invests his money has been sold. Therefore, he has no choice but to sell his investment.

Trading Opportunities Arise

Although the long-term investor has investments he plans to keep for a long time, it can happen that his research shows potential for earning more profits through day trading and swing trading. He may take up some of these opportunities, although these trades will surely put his portfolio at risk.

Short Selling Opportunities Arise

Lastly, a long-term investor can also take advantage of short selling if he sees an asset's decline in price. He normally borrows the asset from his broker then sells it. If the price further goes down, he buys back the asset and pays his broker. He keeps the price difference as his profit. Short selling, however, is an expensive endeavor because interest has to be paid to the broker. Thus, it is a strategy used primarily for short-term trading.

The price of the asset can also go up unexpectedly. Thus it is possible for the trader to lose money. To avoid this risk, he must do his research carefully before deciding to short sell a financial asset. Short selling can be profitable especially to those traders who do a lot of careful research and don't mind additional risks.

Chapter 11: Entry Strategies for the New Day Trader

There are three tools a day trader can use in identifying his entry points. In his analysis, he can use the intra-day candlestick charts to learn about the asset's price action. If he wants to see orders as they are executed, then he can check Level II Quotes and ECN. Lastly, he can monitor news about his financial assets through the real-time news service.

Intra-day Candlestick Pattern

A day trader can check out different candlestick patterns to determine his entry points. But, the most reliable pattern is the doji reversal pattern. To confirm the existence of this pattern, the day trader looks for spikes in the volume because it will say if the traders support the price level. He then searches for prior support at that level by looking at the prior high of the day or low of the day. Lastly, he looks at the Level II situation, which shows every open order and its size. By following these steps, the day trader can find out if the doji can pave the way for a turnaround or not. If conditions are favorable, then he makes an entry position.

The determination of the price target, however, is dependent on his trading style.

Scalping

Scalping is trading profitably by selling the financial asset as soon as the preset price level is reached. The price target is set right after profitability is reached.

Fading

Fading is short selling the financial asset as soon as there is a rapid price movement upward. However, it is assumed that current buyers are scared, and early buyers are cashing out for the profits, and the financial asset is overbought. This strategy is very risky yet very rewarding. The price target is set when buyers begin to move again.

Daily Pivots

In using this strategy, the day trader makes a profit by taking advantage of the financial asset's daily volatility. He buys at the low of the day and sells at the high of the day. The price target is set at the next reversal.

Momentum

The day trader relies on trending moves or news releases. He buys based on the news and sells when there are signs of reversal. The price target is set when there's a decrease in volume, as well as when bearish candles begin to appear.

Chapter 12: Exit Strategies for the New Day Trader

Stop-loss Determination

Trading on margin can open the day trader to a lot of vulnerabilities due to steep price movements. Therefore, it is important for him to set a stop-loss strategy. Some day traders have 2 stop-losses. The mental stop-loss is set when the price level makes a turnaround unexpectedly. This means that the day trader has to exit immediately. The physical stop-loss, on the other hand, is the price level that determines the point at which the day trader can still tolerate losses.

Most retail day traders also set a daily maximum loss amount which they are willing to lose. When this amount has been reached, day traders often stop trading for the day. A new day trader must follow this strategy so that he doesn't take any further risks when he continues to trade even if he has reached his maximum loss amount.

Continuous Evaluation and Development of Trading Strategy

The reality is that a lot of day traders lose a lot of money. There is no truth to the belief that a day trader can earn as much as thrice his capital yearly without exerting a lot of effort. It is possible to get rich in day trading if the trader has a well-defined trading strategy in order to improve the odds of generating huge profits.

It is necessary for the day trader to evaluate his performance based on how well he follows his trading plan. It isn't necessary to focus on making money. What the day trader needs is for him to determine trading problems he may have and to find solutions for them.

Chapter 13: Day Trading Costs

A serious day trader must consider the costs of trading. Some of them even hire the services of an accountant to help them with tax preparation. As expenses begin to pile up, it is important to keep track of them for taxation purposes because there are items that are tax deductible. It is a great practice to be mindful of investment expenses.

Tax-Deductible Expenses:

Accounting, clerical, and legal fees - A day trader may need to hire the services of an attorney when he sets up his day trading career. He may need to pay his accountant to help him with tax matters, as well as to explain to him investment expenses to help him evaluate his day trading strategies. It is good to know that professional fees can be deducted from his investment income.

Investment advice and counsel - Some advice and counsel are allowed to be deducted from the investment income. Such tax-deductible items include research services, newspapers, magazines, and books that help the day trader define his trading strategy. Any fee paid for investment advisory is also tax deductible.

Investment interest - Interest paid on investment loans is tax deductible. However, this amount may be negligible especially if the day trader only borrows money for a few hours.

Office expenses - A day trader who trades in an office can deduct expenses such as rent from his investment income. Expenses from the home office are also tax deductible. However, he must ensure that such expenses really pertain to his day trading business. Office supplies and equipment are also tax deductible if such items are used for trading 50% of the time.

Safe deposit box rental - If the deposit box is used to store investment documents, then the rent can be deducted from investment income. If the box is also used to store other items, then only a part of the rent can be deducted.

State income taxes - Taxes paid to the state are deductible from investment income. However, only state income taxes pertaining to the day trading activities can be deducted. In most cases, government bond transactions are already tax-exempt and are therefore not tax deductible. Every state has a different rule in investment income. As such, the day trader can hire an accountant to help him.

Expenses That Aren't Tax-Deductible

Commission - An amount paid to the broker that isn't tax deductible. However, it can be added to the other costs and subtracted from the trade's proceeds. It isn't subject to the limitations on expenses that are tax deductible. Also, transfer taxes levied on securities are treated the same as commissions.

Investment seminars - Such seminars can help the day trader become better in his trading career. However, expenses incurred in attending these seminars aren't tax deductible.

Stockholder's meetings - Day traders won't find any use in attending stockholder's meetings. For long-term investors, these meetings offer insights to the firm's plans. Costs incurred relating to attendance of stockholder's meetings aren't tax deductible.

Chapter 14: How to Compute Expected Profit For the Day

There are various numbers the day trader needs to know in order to compute how much his expected profit will be. First, he has to know how many losing trades he has for the day. Second, he has to find out how much his average percentage loss on a single losing trade is. Third, he has to know how many winning trades he has in one trading day. Lastly, he has to find out how much his average percentage gain per winning trade is.

For example, the day trader loses 40% of the time and his average loss is 1%. Therefore, he wins 60% of the time with a 1.5% average gain. To compute the expected profit per trade, the formula is:

Percentage of losing trade × average percentage loss + percentage of winning trades × average percentage gain.

In the example, the expected profit per trade is 0.005. This means that the day trader earns 0.05% on every trade. If he makes more trades, the average earnings can increase. However, one can't discount the probability of loss.

Chapter 15: How to Accumulate Day Trading Profits

Not only does a day trader need to know how much his investment will be, it is also important for him to know what he can do with his profits. A successful day trader has three options. He can also combine these options for the best results.

Compound Interest

This concept is fairly simple. A day trader needs to add his profits to his trading account so that it increases in size and therefore earns bigger profits. Although the trading account doesn't earn interest, a day trader who adds the profits back can generate more profits. The trading account is expected to grow over time. A small-time day trade can benefit a lot from this practice because it builds his account which allows him to take more important trading positions over time.

Pyramid Power

This means a day trader can borrow heavily against his trading profits in order to earn more profits. It is a common practice in every trading session during which a day trader uses his unrealized profits as collateral for loans that he can use to open new trading positions. The process gets repeated during the session until the close of the trading day. This scheme can be very profitable if the financial market moves positively.

However, it is very possible for the plan to collapse if only one of the open positions doesn't do well. The broker usually makes a margin call in case the scheme collapses. There is increased risk in pyramiding power, but the potential return also increases.

Regular Withdrawals

Some day traders withdraw their profits and invest them to a safer long-term investment. They make regular withdrawals and put them into real estate, mutual funds, or government bonds. This way, they are assured of less stress and fear than what usually goes with day trading. Small-time traders usually set aside 10% of their quarterly profits and transfer them to safer investments.

Conclusion

Day trading is a profitable yet very risky strategy. It isn't for the faint-hearted or those who can't handle stress. An individual who wants to pursue day trading must make an effort to study the ins and outs of the trade first before trading full-time. He mustn't be afraid to lose heavily at the start of his career because he won't learn if he doesn't try.

He must be able to decide which strategies fit his trading style in order to generate more profits. He mustn't be afraid to make necessary changes if needed because it is only through continuous monitoring and development of a fitting trading strategy that a day trader be rewarded generously.

I hope this book was able to help you to appreciate and understand day trading.

Finally, if you enjoyed this book, please take the time to share your thoughts and post a review on Amazon. It would be greatly appreciated!

Finally, we would like to ask you to give a short, honest, and unbiased review of this book.

Please & Thank you!

Instant Access to Free Book Package!

As a thank you for the purchase of this book, I want to offer you some more material. We collaborate with multiple other authors specializing in various fields. We have best-selling, master writers in history, biographies, DIY projects, home improvement, arts & crafts and much more! **We make a promise to you to deliver at least 4 books a week in different genres, a value of $20-30, for FREE!**

All you need to do is sign up your email here at http://nextstopsuccess.net/freebooks/ to join our Book Club. You will get weekly notification for more free books, courtesy of the First Class Book Club.

As a special thank you, we don't want you to wait until next week for these 4 free books. We want to give you 4 **RIGHT NOW**.

Here's what you will be getting:

- A fitness book called "BOSU Workout Routine Made Easy!"
- A book on Jim Rohn, a master life coach: "The Best of Jim Rohn: Lessons for Life Changing Success"
- A detailed biography on Conan O'Brien, a favorite late night TV show host.
- A World War 2 Best Selling box set (2 books in 1!): "The Third Reich: Nazi Rise & Fall + World War 2: The Untold Secrets of Nazi Germany".

To get instant access to this free ebook package (a value of $25), and weekly free material, all you need to do is click the link below:

http://nextstopsuccess.net/freebooks/

Add us on Facebook: First Class Book Club

www.ingramcontent.com/pod-product-compliance
Lightning Source LLC
Chambersburg PA
CBHW070430190526
45169CB00003B/1492